Paul Leicester Ford

The Origin, Purpose and Result of the Harrisburg Convention

of 1788

A Study in Popular Government

Paul Leicester Ford

The Origin, Purpose and Result of the Harrisburg Convention of 1788
A Study in Popular Government

ISBN/EAN: 9783337112240

Printed in Europe, USA, Canada, Australia, Japan

Cover: Foto ©Suzi / pixelio.de

More available books at **www.hansebooks.com**

THE

ORIGIN, PURPOSE AND RESULT

OF THE

HARRISBURG CONVENTION OF 1788.

A

STUDY IN POPULAR GOVERNMENT

BY

PAUL LEICESTER FORD.

"In our Government the real power lies in the majority of the community and the invasion of . . . rights is chiefly to be apprehended, not from the acts of Government contrary to the sense of its constituents, but from the acts in which the Government is the mere instrument of the major number of the constituents."—*Madison.*

BROOKLYN, N. Y.
1890.

In spite of the universal acceptance of majority rule as the basis and inherent principle of all government in the United States, there have been few instances in our history when this power has been able to govern according to its inclination. From the earliest period, both our laws and their administration have been for the most part a series of compromises between the majority and the minority; and the few attempts actually made by the former to govern the latter with a high hand, have usually resulted either in a secession of the minority or in a reaction which reversed or moderated the policy of our plastic and changing ruler.

No better illustration of this forced concession of the dominant party, to the will of the minority, is to be found, than in the history of the ratifications by the states, of our national constitution. The necessity for union in Delaware, Georgia, New Jersey, and Connecticut, was so strong that practically there was unanimity in the conventions of those states. In the states of Massachusetts, South Carolina, New Hampshire, Virginia, and New York, the ratifications were only carried after mutual concessions. In the Maryland

convention,

convention, though the vote for adoption was over five
to one, the majority so far yielded to the wishes of the
minority as to appoint a committee to prepare amendments, and only refused to carry out this compromise,
when an ulterior motive was discovered. Thus in
Pennsylvania alone did the Federal majority refuse
concessions to the anti-Federal minority; and the resulting action of the minority is of value as a study
in popular government.

The interests of the populous part of Pennsylvania
made the state in favor of federal union, and to this
natural advantage was added the influence of her
ablest men, as well as the possession of a majority in
favor of union in the legislature. This latter advantage enabled the Federalist party to act before the
opposition, whose strength lay in the agricultural and
western counties, could plan and organize their resistance. Yet in the state, at least three causes existed
to produce an obstinate opposition.

I. The so called Constitutional party, or those who
favored the constitution under which the state was
then governed, were firmly seated in the council,
which was not merely the state executive, but had
control of all the state patronage. It therefore dreaded
any change which would either risk its supremacy,

or

or lessen the offices and powers of the state government.

II. A fear in the agricultural population, that a national government would not merely bring an increase of taxation, but would, by its power over commerce, unduly raise the price of commodities, and favor the merchant and trading classes who then formed the leading element of our cities, and whom the rural populations regarded as "blood-suckers," living off the farming interest.

III. A suspicion, on the part of the counties west of the Alleghanies, that the treaty power of Congress would be used to bargain the navigation of the Mississippi for commercial privileges advantageous to the coast states; and an equal fear, on the part of certain vested institutions, that this same power would be employed to take from them and restore to their original owners, the properties declared forfeited from the loyalists during the revolutionary war.*

---

* It is only fair to state that Prof. McMaster and Mr. Stone, in their admirable work, *Pennsylvania and the Federal Constitution*, find the cause of this opposition in the fact that "the constitution proposed for the United States was in many ways the direct opposite of the constitution of Pennsylvania. . . . In opposing the new plan these men simply opposed a system of government which, if adopted, would force

That

6

That this opposition took different grounds in the public discussion, was really a matter of necessity. Powerful though these motives were, they were too mercenary to publicly appeal to the people on. Except for the question of taxation, they are not even mentioned in the lengthy discussions in the legislature and the convention, nor in the newspaper arguments with which the press teemed for nearly a twelve-month. The lack of a bill of rights; of a guarantee of trial by jury, and liberty of the press; the dangers arising from the federal courts; the great expenses of the proposed government, and the resulting heavy taxation; and, finally, the eventual destruction of the state governments, with a consequent loss if not annihilation of personal liberty—these were the phantasies with which the "Antis" sought to raise the people against its adoption.

That this opposition came from very different causes

---

them to undo a piece of work done with great labor and beheld with great pride and satisfaction." But I can see no more necessity of their undoing their state constitution than there was for Georgia, which had much the same government ; and am convinced that so bitter and determined an opposition could not have, in so short a time, arisen on such abstract questions as the singleness or plurality of the legislative and executive powers.

than

than these ostensible ones, is proved by its first organization. Before the constitution was even made
public or its clauses known, a meeting had been held
at Judge George Bryan's, in Philadelphia, to concert
measures of opposition, and the knowledge of this was
unquestionably one reason why the Federalists treated
their opponents' reasonings and wishes with so little
regard, and adopted what a leading Anti-federalist
termed their "system of precipitancy."*

The legislature, with its Federal majority, aided by
the citizens of Philadelphia, who were even more
Federal in sentiment, passed resolutions for an early
convention, without listening to the protests of the
minority. As a consequence, the latter drew up and
published an "Address," and at once began an attack
not merely on the constitution, but a personal one on
its framers and advocates. But they fought at a dis-
advantage, for their strength, as already stated, lay in
the western and agricultural counties, and communication was too slow to enable them to organize and
win converts in the short time given them before the
elections for the members of the convention.

As a result of this unfairness, so the Anti-federalists

---

* John Smilie.

claimed,

claimed, only a trifle over one-sixth of those qualified, voted on the candidates for the convention,* of whom the Federalists elected forty-six and the Antis twenty-three. When the convention assembled, therefore, it was with the full belief on the part of the opposition, that it did not represent "the voice of the people of Pennsylvania,"† and they plead for an adjournment which would give time for public opinion to declare itself. Defeated in this, they next adopted the tactics of speaking against time, and practiced it so successfully that three of them were accused of having cost the state one thousand pounds in discussing the words

---

* "The election for members of the Convention was held at so early a period, and the want of information was so great, that some of us did not know of it until it was over, and we have reason to believe that great numbers of the people of Pennsylvania have not yet had an opportunity of sufficiently examining the proposed Constitution. . . . On examining the number of votes given for members of the present State convention, we find that of upwards of *seventy thousand* freemen who are entitled to vote in Pennsylvania, the whole convention has been elected by *thirteen thousand* voters, and though *two-thirds* of the members of the convention have thought proper to ratify the proposed Constitution, yet these *two-thirds* were elected by the votes of only *six thousand and eight hundred* freemen."—*Address and Reasons of Dissent of the Minority of the Convention of the State of Pennsylvania to their Constituents.*

† John Smilie.

"annihilation"

"annihilation" and "consolidation."* Finally the majority gave up trying to placate them and voted to ratify, even refusing to allow the minority to enter a protest on the minutes.

In another way, too, the Federalists increased the bitterness of their opponents. Of the eleven papers then published in the state, but three were printed outside of Philadelphia, and they had but limited circulation. On the Philadelphia papers, therefore, were the Anti-federalists compelled to depend for the publication of their views, but these were not only, with but two exceptions, under Federalist views, but all found the bulk of their readers in town, where the popular feeling, as expressed by the vote, was nearly eight to one for the constitution. The Federalists, therefore, by threats, by withdrawing their subscriptions, and by other methods, endeavored, and to a certain extent succeeded, in closing these papers to the opposition, and secured the suppression of the debates of the convention, except what they chose should be printed. So also, by bribery of the post-boys, the Anti-federal newspapers from other states were largely excluded, and so knowledge of the opposition elsewhere kept from them.

---

* Pennsylvania Gazette, Dec. 19, 1787.

Refused

Refused all concessions by what they deemed a minority, bound to a government by acts which they claimed were "irregular," with press and mail under the influence of their enemies, the so-called minority saw clearly that their opposition must adopt new methods of warfare. The ratification by the convention was final so far as regarded legal acts; but they claimed that the Federalists had instituted what amounted to a revolution, and so probably justified their own acts to themselves, if they even deemed justification necessary.

The convention dissolved on December 13th, and five days after, twenty-one of the twenty-three members of the minority of the convention united in signing and publishing: *An Address and Reasons of Dissent of the Minority of the Convention of the State of Pennsylvania to their Constituents.** Colored, if not drafted by Richard Henry Lee, of Virginia, it was intended to present in small compass all the Antifederal objections both to the Federal convention, the constitution, and the Pennsylvania convention.

But the chief value of this address is not the objections to the constitution, but in the position its publi-

---

* Printed as a broad sheet, Dec. 18, 1787.

cation

cation placed the minority—a position which has been most strangely overlooked by every historian who has written of the matter. The battle was over, and apparently irrevocably lost, yet the Anti-Federalists were crying aloud to the people of the state:

"It remains with you whether you will think those inestimable privileges, which you have so ably contended for, should be sacrificed at the shrine of despotism, or whether you mean to contend for them with the same spirit that has so often baffled the attempts of an aristocratic faction to rivet the shackles of slavery on you and your unborn posterity."

This amounted to a notice by the "Antis" that opposition had not and was not to cease. Yet any appeal now to the people could only mean either an attempt to secure a new convention, which should reverse the action of the former one, with the danger that the new government would not recognize such an act, or an opposition that threatened to take unconstitutional steps towards preventing the union of Pennsylvania with the other states under the proposed system.

Strangely enough, in spite of this formidable outlook, the press of the period remained absolutely silent. No warning note of the new battle this address gave notice of, was sounded publicly. But that

that the Federalists quickly realized that an ill-gained
battle in popular government must soon be fought
over again, is shown by a letter of Benjamin Rush,*
who but two months earlier had been one of the most
uncompromising and extreme leaders for the "system
of precipitancy," and which read as follows:

. . . It is now generally agreed that if we had not
been so hasty in our determination, the opposition
would have been less violent. Already the ill effects
are manifest, and a united effort is to be apprehended,
which may give a different character to the proceedings. The counties in the western part of the state
are most to be feared, for the Connecticut claimants
are opposed to any government, and many of the inhabitants fear so much the action of the new government concerning the subject most interesting to our
settlements on the Ohio, that they are disposed to cast
in their lot with them. . . .

But for the season of the year, which precluded organization, the Federalists would have had more
cause for worry; but fortunately for them, the mail
could not be trusted, and all other communication
was so poor and uncertain that the frost must be out
of the ground before this opposition could more than
arrange its plans in Philadelphia.

* To Hugh Williamson, Feb. 16, 1788.

And

And what were these plans? The sole light I have been able to find on them, is given in a letter* of Judge George Bryan, the great head and front of the Anti-Federalists in Pennsylvania, to George Clinton, Governor of New York. Calling first for a united opposition to the constitution, he then writes:

. . . As soon as the Season permit, we plan to hold at some convenient point a Meeting of Delegates who shall decide how far the Majority of the People of this State are to abide by the decision of the violent and tyranus [sic] Minority. Our action will much depend on the Complexion of the Acts of those States which we look to to hold up the Standard of Liberty—and I must beg that you will write me, by Mr. Aldis, who returns to this City shortly, of the probable action of your State, and that you will keep me informed of any change in Sentiment. . . .

When this letter was written, the snow lay on the ground, and the news of the ratification by Massachusetts had not reached Philadelphia. But four states† besides Pennsylvania had ratified, and none of them were important. It was confidently believed by the Anti-Federalists that Virginia and New York would

---

* Feb. 9, 1788.

† Delaware, New Jersey, Georgia and Connecticut.

reject

reject the constitution. With their moral support, the Pennsylvania Anti-Federalists clearly believed it still possible to prevent her union with the remaining states.

For over four months the project remained quiescent, so far as I have been able to discover. It is true that "Centinel" and "Philadelphiensis"* still continued to attack Federal measures and men through the press, striving to make both odious to the people; but during that period nothing of the proposed convention is discoverable, unless the mention in the hereinafter printed letter to the "Societies in Each County as have already been formed for Political Purposes," can be treated as such †—a delay as unaccountable, as it was fatal, to any project involving what was clearly wished for by those who planned it. For in that period five important states ‡ gave their consent to the

---

* The letters of "Centinel" were, by his own statement, written by Samuel Bryan, son of the George Bryan who figures so prominently in this whole movement, and unquestionably therefore represent his father's views. Those signed "Philadelphiensis" were written by Benjamin Workman, a tutor in the University of Pennsylvania, one of those vested institutions already alluded to.

† See infra, page 191.

‡ Massachusetts, Maryland, South Carolina, New Hampshire, and Virginia.

new

new government, making its organization a certainty, and a resistance to it treason.

Finally, in July, the work of the "Anti-Federal Junto" in Philadelphia first became obvious in Cumberland county. One of the central counties, it had early distinguished itself by sending to the Pennsylvania convention petitions signed by some seven hundred and fifty inhabitants against the constitution; and for these two reasons was presumably selected by the Philadelphia workers for the inauguration of their schemes. To various well known Anti-Federalists throughout the state a circular letter with enclosures was sent, which read as follows:

EAST PENNSBOROUGH, CUMBERLAND,
JULY 3, 1788.

Sir: That ten states have already unexpectedly, without amending, ratified the constitution proposed for the government of these United States, cannot have escaped the notice of the friends of liberty. That the way is prepared for the full organization of the government, with all its foreseen and consequent dangers, is too evident, and unless prudent steps be taken to combine the friends to amendments in some plan in which they can confidently draw together, and exert their power in unison, the liberty of the American citizens must lie at the discretion of Congress, and most

most probably posterity become slaves to the officers of government.

The means adopted and proposed by a meeting of delegates from the townships of this county for preventing the alleged evils, and also the calamities of a civil war, are, as may be observed in perusing the proceedings of the said meeting herewith transmitted, to request such persons as shall be judged fit within the counties respectively, to use their influence to obtain a meeting of delegates from each township, to take into consideration the necessity of amending the constitution of these United States, and for that purpose to nominate and appoint a number of delegates to represent the county in a general conference of the counties of this commonwealth, to be held at Harrisburg on the third day of September next, then and there to devise such amendments, and such mode of obtaining them, as in the wisdom of the delegates shall be judged most satisfactory and expedient.

A law will, no doubt, be soon enacted by the General Assembly for electing eight members to represent this State in the new Congress. It will, therefore, be expedient to have proper persons put in nomination by the delegates in conference, being the most likely method of directing the voices of the electors to the same object and of obtaining the desired end.

The Society, of which you are chairman, is requested to call a meeting agreeable to the foregoing designs, and lay before the delegates the proceedings of this county,

county, to the intent that the State may unite in casting off the yoke of slavery, and once more establish union and liberty.

By order of the meeting, I am, with real esteem, sir,
Your most obedient servant,

BENJAMIN BLYTH, *Chairman.**

———

CUMBERLAND COUNTY,
JULY 3d, 1788.

Dr. Sir: You are Earnestly requested to call a meeting of some of the best informed men of your County from Each Township with Design to consider of the necessity of sending Delegates from the Countys to Represent you in a General Conference of the State in Order to conclude upon such Amendments and such mode of Obtaining them as the Conference in their wisdom may Judge Proper the time and place of Meeting is, as you will see by our Resolutions the necessity of the measure need not be urged. Confiding in your Friendship & Integrity we hope you will Exert yourself for the good of Mankind.

BENJ'N BLYTH, C. M.

———

AT MR. JAMES BELL'S ———.

In a meeting of Delegates from the Several Townships of the Beforesaid County Benj'n Blyth—in the chair, called for the purpose of advising the most eli-

———

* From *Pennsylvania and the Federal Convention*, p. 552.

gible

gible mode of obtaining such Amendments in the Constitution proposed by the General Convention for the Government of these United States as may remove the causes of jealousy and fear of a Tyranical Aristocracy, the foundation of which appears to be in many parts of the said Constitution, and Secure and hand Down to Posterity the Blessings of Dear bought Freedom; and thereby most cordially engage each State and Every Citizen, not only for wrath but Conscience sake, to aid and support the officers of the Government in the due Executive thereof; after seriously considering the importance of the subject and the Duty of Citizens; have come to the following Resolutions, viz.: Resolved, that it is the opinion of this meeting that the Constitution proposed by the General Convention of the United States is in several parts Destructive of that Liberty for which so much blood and Treasure has been spent, and Subversion of the Several State Governments by which the Rights and Liberties of the People have been guarded and secured. That it is the Indispensable Duty of Every Citizen to use all the lawfull means to obtain such Amendments in the said Constitution or take such measures as shall be necessary for the Security of Religion and Liberty.—Resolved, that it is the opinion of the members of this meeting that it will be Expedient to Collect as Soon and as Accurately as Possible the Sentiments of the Citizens of this State Touching such Amendments and such mode of obtaining them as shall be to the said

Citizens

Citizens most agreeable.—Resolved, that in order to effectuate the foregoing Resolutions that a Circular Letter be written and signed by the Chairman, and Addressed to such Societys in each County as have already been formed for Political purposes, and to such as shall be formed in any county where none is yet formed, or to such persons as shall be judged fit, requesting that measures be Taken to call a meeting of Delegates from Each Township within the respective Counties, to meet as soon as conveniently may be and take into consideration the necessity and propriety of Amending the Constitution of the United States, and for that purpose to Appoint Delegates to meet in a General Conference of the State at Harrisburgh on the Third Day of September, 1788—then and there to Consider and Devise a plan the most Likely to Succeed in Obtaining the desired Amendment—Resolved by the meeting, that five members be chosen by the County Cumberland, or three out of the five to represent said County in the Conference to be held at Harrisburgh the 3d Day of Sept 1788—the place and time aforesaid.

B. BLYTH, C. M.‡

---

‡ Addressed and endorsed "John Nicholson, Esquire, Comptroller General, Phila."—Letter from Benjamin Blythe, Esqr., C. M., Rec'd Aug. 20th, 1788—Answered Aug. 20th." On the blank sheet is written, " Sir, you will be punctual in laying these resolutions before yʳ committee ; if there are any such in the city, and use your endeavors

The

The whole tone of these papers shows how far events had modified the program of those opposed to the new government. But this was even further modified by the news that New York had ratified the Constitution, which reached Pennsylvania before the towns could act on the suggestions of this letter. Of their proceedings and action, but one example is left to us, but was presumably a fair sample of them all:

NEWTOWN, AUGUST 15, 1788.

Gentlemen: The important crisis now approaching (confident I am you will think with me) demands the most serious attention of every friend of American liberty. The Constitution of the United States is now adopted by eleven States in the Union, and no doubt the other two will follow their example; for however just the sentiments of the opposition may be, I do conceive it would be the height of madness and folly and in fact a crime of very detrimental consequence to our country, to refuse to acquiesce in a measure received in form by so great a majority of our country; not only to ourselves individually, but to the community at large—for the worst that we can expect from a bad form of government is anarchy and confusion, with all

---

that they comply with the same." John Nicholson, Esq'. C. Gen'l. From the original Ms. in the possession of Mr. Gordon L. Ford, of Brooklyn, N. Y.

its

its common train of grievances—and by an opposition
in the present situation of affairs we are sure of it.
On the other hand by a sullen and inactive conduct, it
will give the promoters and warm advocators of the
plan an opportunity (if such design they have) to
shackle us with these manacles, that we fear may be
formed under color of the law, and we be led to know
it is constitutional, when it is too late to extricate ourselves and posterity from bondage.

To you it is not worth while to animadvert on the
plain and pointed tendency the constitution has to this
effect, and how easily it may be accomplished in
power under its influence. That virtue is not the
standard that has principally animated the adoption of
the constitution in this State, I believe, is too true.
Let us, therefore, as we wish to serve our country, and
show the world that those only who have wished
amendments were truly federal, adopt the conduct of
our fellow-citizens in the back counties. Let us as
freemen, call a meeting of those citizens who wish for
amendments, in a committee of the county, delegated
from each township, for the purpose expressed in
a copy of the (circular) enclosed. In promoting a
scheme of this kind, I hope we shall not only have the
satisfaction of seeing the minds and exertions of all
who wish for amendments centre in this object, which
will swallow others more injurious, but we will enjoy
the supreme felicity of having assisted in snatching
from slavery a once happy and worthy people.

I therefore

I therefore hope you will undertake to call together your township, have delegates chosen to represent them in a committee to be held in the house of George Piper, on Monday, the 21st inst., at nine o'clock in the forenoon, for the purpose of appointing delegates to represent them in the State conference, and for giving them instructions, etc.

If you should apprehend the people will not call a town-meeting for the purpose, that you will, as we intend here, write or call upon a few of the most respectable people of your township to attend at the general meeting, as they intend to do at Philadelphia, if they cannot accomplish their purpose in any other way.

Your usual public spirit on occasions of this kind, I am sure, needs no spur. We shall therefore rest assured that we will meet a representation of the township committed to your charge on the day appointed.

I am with every sentiment of esteem,

(Signed.)   Yours etc.,
JAMES HANNA.

To John Vandegrift, Esq., Captain Nathan Vansant, and Mr. Jacob Vandegrift. Bensalem.*

Bucks County, State of Pennsylvania, August 25, 1788.

The ratification of the federal constitution and its expected operation, forming a new æra in the American world, and giving cause of hope to some and fear

---

* From *Pennsylvania and the Federal Constitution*, p. 553.

to

to others; it has been thought proper that the freemen of the State, or delegates chosen by them, should meet together and deliberate on the subject. Accordingly it has been proposed, that a meeting of deputies from the different counties be held at Harrisburg the 3d day of September next. A circular letter bearing the above proposition was sent to this county, and in pursuance thereof, there met this day at Piper's tavern, in Bedminster township, the following gentlemen from the townships annexed to their names respectively:

Newtown,	James Hanna, Esquire.
Warwick,	John Crawford,
	Hugh Ramsay,
	Capt. William Walker,
	Benjamin Snodgrass,
	Samuel Flack.
Newbritain,	James Snodgrass,
	Thomas Stewart,
	David Thomas.
Bedminster,	Jacob Utt,
	Alexander Hughes,
	George Piper,
	Daniel Soliday.
Haycock,	Capt. Manus Yost,
	John Keller.
Rockhill,	Samuel Smith, Esquire.
Millford,	Henry Blilaz,
	Henry Hoover.
	Springfield,

Springfield,	Colonel John Smith,
	Charles Fleming.
Durham,	Richard Backhouse, Esquire.
Tunicum,	John Thompson,
	Jacob Weaver,
	George Bennet.
Nockamixon,	Samuel Willson,
	George Vogle.
Richland,	Benjamin Seagle.
Plumstead,	Thomas Wright,
	Thomas Gibson,
	James Ruckman,
	Major John Shaw,
	James Farres,
	Thomas Henry,
	Moses Kelly,
	Henry Geddis.
Warrington,	Rev. Nathaniel Erwin,
	Captain William Walker.
Buckingham,	Captain Samuel Smith.
Solesbury,	Henry Seabring.
Hilltown,	Joseph Grier.

Samuel Smith, Esq., chosen Chairman, and James Hanna, Esq., Secretary. After some time spent in discussing the business of the meeting, Resolved, that the Reverend Nathaniel Erwin, Richard Backhouse, Samuel Smith, John Crawford, and James Hanna, Esquires, be a committee to draw resolves expressive

of

of the sense of this meeting on the subject before them.

In a short time thereafter the following were presented by the gentlemen appointed, and unanimously approved:

Resolved 1. That it is the opinion of this meeting that the plan of government for the United States, formed by the general convention, having been adopted by eleven of the States, ought in conformity to the resolves of said convention, to come into operation, and have force until altered in a constitutional way

2. That as we mean to act the part of peaceable citizens ourselves, so we will support the said plan of government and those who act under it, against all illegal violence.

3. That the said plan of government will admit of very considerable amendments, which ought to be made in the mode pointed out in the constitution itself.

4. That as few governments once established have ever been altered in favor of liberty, without confusion and bloodshed, the requisite amendments in said constitution ought to be attempted as soon as possible.

5. That we will use our utmost endeavours in a pacific way to procure such alterations in the federal constitution as may be necessary to secure the rights and liberties of ourselves and posterity.

6. That we approve of a state meeting being held at Harrisburg the third day of September next, on the subject of the above resolves.

7. That

7. That four persons ought to be delegated from
this county to attend said meeting, and join with the
deputies from other counties who may meet with them
(in a recommendation to the citizens of this state) of a
suitable set of men to represent them in the new Congress, and generally to acquiesce and assist in the pro-
motion of such plan or plans as may be designed by
the said state conferrees for the purpose of obtaining
the necessary amendments of said constitution, as far
as is consistent with our views, expressed in the foregoing resolves.

Agreeably to the resolve last past, the Reverend
Nathaniel Erwin, Richard Backhouse, John Crawford,
and James Hanna, esquires, or any two of them, were
appointed to represent us in said conference to be held
at Harrisburg.

Resolved, That James Hanna, Esquire, be requested
to hand the foregoing proceedings to the Press for
publication

SAMUEL SMITH, Chairman.*

But if a moderate tone was assumed in public
towards the new government, the extremists were still
not entirely without hope that the coming convention
might refuse to "acquiesce in its organization in this
State." Foremost among these was Albert Gallatin,
then under thirty years of age, and, presumably elected

---

* Independent Gazetteer, Sept. 3, 1788, VII. No 851.

to

to represent the county of Fayette,—one of those which so feared the future action of **Congress on the Mississippi question** that they were "disposed to cast in their lot" with the inhabitants of the future states of Kentucky and Tennessee, which were now loudly talking of independence. He brought with him to the convention, or wrote after his arrival, a series of resolutions which are of the utmost value, in the dearth of material on this convention, as showing with what feelings individual members viewed the proposed meeting, and what their intentions were before, or shortly after their arrival:

. . . We, &c., . . . are united in opinion that a federal government is the only one that can preserve the liberties and secure the happiness of the inhabitants of such an extensive empire as the United States; and experience having taught us that the ties of our Union, under the Articles of Confederation, were so weak as to deprive us of some of the greatest advantages we had a right to expect from such a government, therefore are fully convinced that a more efficient one is absolutely necessary. But at the same time we must declare that although the constitution proposed for the United States is likely to obviate most of the inconveniences we labored under, yet several parts of it appear so exceptionable to us that nothing but the fullest confidence of obtaining a
revision

revision of them by a general convention and our reluctance to enter into any dangerous measures could prevail on us to acquiesce in its organization in this State. We are sensible that a large number of the citizens, both in this and other States, who gave their assent to its being carried in execution previous to any amendments, were actuated more by the fear of the dangers that might arise from any delays than by a conviction of its being perfect. We therefore are convinced that they now will concur with us in pursuing every peaceable method of obtaining a speedy revision of the Constitution in the mode pointed out by the same, and when we reflect on the present situation of the Union we can entertain no doubt that motives of conciliation and the dictates of policy and prudence will conspire to induce every man of true federal principles to give his support to a measure not only calculated to recommend the new constitution to the approbation and support of a numerous class of American citizens, but even necessary to prevent the total defection of some members of the Union.

Strongly impressed with these sentiments, we have resolved as follows:

1. *Resolved*, That in order to prevent a dissolution of the Union and to secure our liberties and those of our posterity, it is necessary that a revision of the Federal Constitution be obtained in the most speedy manner

2. That the safest manner to obtain such a revision will

will be in conformity to the request of the State of New York, to use our endeavors to have a federal convention called as soon as possible.

3. That in order that the friends to amendments of the Federal Constitution who are inhabitants of this State may act in concert, it is necessary, and it is hereby recommended to the several counties in the State, to appoint committees who may correspond, one with the other, and with such similar committees as may be formed in other States.

4. That the friends to amendments of the Federal Constitution in the several States be invited to meet in a general Conference to be held at   , on   , and that members be elected by this conference, who or any of them shall meet at said place and time, in order to devise, in concert with such other delegates from the several States as may come under similar appointments, on such amendments to the Federal Constitution as to them may seem most necessary, and on the most likely way to carry them into effect.*

Of the proceedings of the Convention, nothing is known except what they chose to print in the newspapers. But the time had passed when even Gallatin's resolutions could obtain acceptance. " Recommendation " and " petition," not " decision " and " action,"

---

* Henry Adams' *Writings of Albert Gallatin*, I, 1. They are also printed without the very important preamble in *Pennsylvania and the Federal Constitution*.

were

were the only methods left them, and their proceedings read so tamely as to induce all former historians to pass them over in a mere paragraph :—

Harrisburgh, Dauphin County,
State of Pennsylvania,
September 3d, 1788.

Agreeably to a circular letter which originated in the county of Cumberland, inviting to a conference such of the citizens of this State, who conceive that a revision of the federal system, lately proposed for the government of these United States, is necessary; a number of gentlemen from the city of Philadelphia and the counties of Philadelphia, Bucks, Chester, Lancaster, Cumberland, Berks, Northumberland, Bedford, Fayette, Washington, Franklin, Dauphin and Huntingdon, assembled at this place for the said purpose, viz.

Hon. George Bryan, Esq.,
Charles Pettit,
Blair M'Clenachan,
Richard Backhouse,
James Hanna,
Joseph Gardner,
James Mercer,
Benjamin Blyth,
Robert Whitehill,
John Jordan,

William Petriken,
Jonathan Hoge,
John Bishop,
Daniel Montgomery,
John Lytle,
John Dickey,
Honorable John Smiley,
Albert Gallatin,
James Marshall,
Benjamin Elliott,

William

William Sterrett,
William Rodgers,
Adam Orth,
John Rodgers,
Thomas Murray,
Robert M'Kean,
John Kean.

Richard Baird,
James Crooks,
John A. Hanna,
Daniel Bradley,
Robert Smith,
James Anderson,

Blair M'Clenachan,* Esq., was unanimously elected Chairman, and John A. Hanna, Esq., Secretary.

After free discussion and mature deliberation had upon the subject before them, the following resolutions and propositions were adopted :

The ratification of the Federal Constitution having formed a new era in the American world, highly interesting to all the citizens of the United States, it is not less the duty than the privilege of every citizen, to examine with attention the principles and probable effects of a system, on which the happiness or misery of the present as well as future generations, so much depend. In the course of such examination many of the good citizens of the State of Pennsylvania have found their apprehensions excited that the constitution in its present form contains in it some principles which may be perverted to purposes injurious to the rights of free citizens, and some ambiguities which may probably lead to contentions incompatible with order

---

* In A. Boyd Hamilton's *Harrisburg Conference* it is stated that "the first proposition was to make Bryan the presiding officer."

and

and good government: in order to remedy these inconveniences, and to avert the apprehended dangers, it has been thought expedient that delegates, chosen by those who wish for early amendments in the said Constitution, should meet together for the purpose of deliberating on the subject, and uniting in some constitutional plan for obtaining the amendments which they may deem necessary.

We the conferees assembled, for the purpose aforesaid, agree in opinion :

That a federal government only can preserve the liberties and secure the happiness of the inhabitants of a country so extensive as these United States; and experience having taught us that the ties of our union, under the articles of confederation, were so weak as to deprive us of some of the greatest advantges we had a right to expect from it. We are fully convinced that a more efficient government is indispensably necessary; but although the Constitution proposed for the United States is likely to obviate most of the inconveniences we labored under; yet several parts of it appear so exceptionable to us, that we are clearly of opinion considerable amendments are essentially necessary : In full confidence, however, of obtaining a revision of such exceptionable parts by a General Convention, and from a desire to harmonize with our fellow citizens, we are induced to acquiesce in the organization of the said Constitution.

We are sensible that a large number of the citizens
both

both in this and the other States, who gave their assent to its being carried into execution, previous to any amendments, were actuated more by the fear of the dangers that might arise from delays, than by a conviction of its being perfect; we therefore hope they will concur with us in pursuing every peaceable method of obtaining a speedy revision of the Constitution in the mode therein provided; and when we reflect on the present circumstances of the union, we can entertain no doubt that motives of conciliation, and the dictates of policy and prudence, will conspire to induce every man of true federal principles, to give his support to a measure which is not only calculated to recommend the new Constitution to the approbation and support of every class of citizens, but even necessary to prevent the total defection of some members of the union.

Strongly impressed with these sentiments, we have agreed to the following resolutions:

1. *Resolved*, That it be recommended to the people of this State to acquiesce in the organization of the said government; but although we thus accord in its organization, we by no means lose sight of the grand object of obtaining very considerable amendments and alterations, which we consider essential to preserve the peace and harmony of the union, and those invaluable privileges for which so much blood and treasure have been recently expended.

2. *Resolved*, That it is necessary to obtain a speedy revision of said Constitution by a general convention.

3. *Resolved*,

3. *Resolved*, That in order to effect this desirable end, a petition be presented to the Legislature of this State, requesting that honorable body to take the earliest opportunity to make application for that purpose to the new Congress.

The petition proposed is as follows:

To the Honorable the Representatives of the Freemen of the Commonwealth of Pennsylvania, in General Assembly met.

The Petition and Representation of the Subscribers, HUMBLY SHEW,

That your petitioners possess sentiments completely federal: being convinced that a confederacy of republican States, and no other, can secure political liberty, happiness and safety throughout a territory so extended as the United States of *America*. They are well apprised of the necessity of devolving extensive powers to Congress, and of vesting the Supreme Legislature with every power and resource of a general nature; and consequently they acquiesce in the general system of government framed by the late *federal convention;* in full confidence, however, that the same will be revised without delay: For however worthy of approbation the general principles and outlines of the said system may be, your petitioners conceive that amendments in some parts of the plan are essential, not only to the preservation of such rights and privileges as ought to be reserved in the respective states, and in
the

the citizens thereof, but to the fair and unembarassed operation of the GOVERNMENT in its various departments. And as provision is made in the *constitution* itself for the making of such amendments as may be deemed necessary; and your petitioners are desirous of obtaining the amendments which occur to them as more immediately desirable and necessary, in the mode admitted by such provision,

They pray that your honorable House, as the Representatives of the people in this Commonwealth, will, in the course of your present session, take such measures as you in your wisdom shall deem most effectual and proper to obtain a revision and amendment of the constitution of the United States, in such parts and in such manner as have been or shall be pointed out by the conventions or assemblies of the respective states; and that such revision be by a general convention of representatives from the several states in the Union.

Your petitioners consider the amendments pointed out in the propositions hereto subjoined as essentially necessary, and as such they suggest them to your notice, submitting to your wisdom the order in which they shall be presented to the consideration of the United States.

The Amendments proposed are as follow,—viz.

1. That Congress shall not exercise any power whatsoever, but such as are expressly given to that body by the constitution of the United States; nor shall

shall any authority, power or jurisdiction, be assumed
or exercised by the executive or judiciary departments
of the union under colour or pretence of construction
or fiction: But all the rights of sovereignty, which
are not by the said constitution expressly and plainly
vested in the Congress, shall be 'deemed to remain
with, and shall be exercised by the several states in
union according to their respective constitutions:
And that every reserve of the rights of individuals,
made by the several constitutions of the states in
union to the citizens and inhabitants of each state
respectively, shall remain inviolate, except so far as
they are expressly and manifestly yielded or narrowed
by the national constitution.

Article 1. Section 2. Paragraph 3.

II. THAT the number of representatives be for the
present, one for every twenty thousand inhabitants
according to the present estimated numbers in the
several states, and continue in that proportion until
the whole number of representatives shall amount to
two hundred; and then to be so proportioned and
modified as not to exceed that number till the proportion of one representative for every thirty thousand
inhabitants, shall amount to the said number of two
hundred.

Section 3.

III. That senators, though chosen for six years,
shall be liable to be recalled, or superseded by other
appointments,

appointments, by the respective Legislatures of the states at any time.

Section 4.

IV. The Congress shall not have power to make or alter regulations concerning the time, place and manner of electing senators and representatives, except in case of neglect or refusal by the state to make regulations for the purpose: and then only for such time as such neglect or refusal shall continue.

Section 8.

V. That when Congress shall require supplies, which are to be raised by direct taxes, they shall demand from the several states their respective quotas thereof, giving a reasonable time to each state to procure and pay the same; and if any state shall refuse, neglect or omit to raise and pay the same within such limited time, then Congress shall have power to assess, levy and collect the quota of such state, together with interest for the same from the time of such delinquency, upon the inhabitants and estates therein, in such manner as they shall by law direct, provided that no poll-tax be imposed.

Section 8.

VI. That no standing army of regular troops shall be raised or kept up in time of peace, without the consent of two-thirds of both Houses in Congress.

Section 8.

VII. That the clause respecting the exclusive legislation

lation over a district not exceeding ten miles square
be qualified by a proviso that such right of legislation
extend only to such regulations as respect the police
and good order thereof.

Article 1. Section 8.

VIII. That each State respectively shall have power
to provide for organizing, arming and disciplining the
militia thereof, whensoever Congress shall omit or
neglect to provide for the same. That the militia
shall not be subject to martial law, but when in actual
service in time of war, invasion or rebellion; and when
not in the actual service of the United States, shall be
subject to such fines, penalties, and punishments only,
as shall be directed or inflicted by the laws of its own
state: nor shall the militia of any state be continued
in actual service longer than two months under any
call of Congress, without the consent of the Legislature
of such state, or, in their recess, the Executive Authority thereof.

Section 9.

IX. That the clause respecting vessels bound to or
from any one of the states, be explained.

Article 3. Section 1.

X. That Congress establish no court other than the
supreme court, except such as shall be necessary for
determining causes of admiralty jurisdiction.

Section 2. Paragraph 2.

XI. That a proviso be added at the end of the
second

second clause of the second section of the third article, to the following effect, viz. Provided, That such appellate jurisdiction, in all cases of common law cognizance, be by Writ of Error, and confined to Matters of Law only ; and that no such writ of error shall be admitted except in revenue cases, unless the matter in controversy exceed the value of three thousand dollars.

Article 6. Paragraph 2.

XII. That to article 6, clause 2, be added the following proviso, viz. Provided always, That no treaty which shall hereafter be made, shall be deemed or construed to alter or affect any law of the United States, or any particular state, until such treaty shall have been laid before and assented to by the House of Representatives in Congress.

Resolved, That the foregoing proceedings be committed to the Chairman for publication.

BLAIR M'CLENACHAN, Chairman.

Attest. JOHN A. HANNA, Secretary.*

That this convention, gathered from the long distances and over the bad roads traveled by the members, only to prepare a Petition that they never even presented to the Assembly,† or to only sound an echo to the recommendations of the convention of New York, is hardly to be believed. After the danger was

---

* From *The Independent Gazetteer*, Sept. 15, 1788, VIII, No. 861.

† In neither the proceedings of the Pennsylvania Assembly or Council is there the slightest reference to this petition.

over, the Federalists spoke of it as " the smuggling
business which took place at Harrisburg with the ostensible purpose of procuring amendments to the constitution, but in fact to form a ticket for representatives
to Congress," * but they dared no such sneer before
the convention had separated. For what it gathered
I have endeavored to show. " The meeting at Harrisburg is represented by its friends as having been con-
ducted with much harmony and moderation," wrote
Madison. † But for the bad roads and snows of that
winter of 1787–88, could this have been written? All
who have studied our constitutional history during
this period must realize by what light balances the
deciding states were induced to ratify, and what violent
resistance to the new government in Pennsylvania
would have involved. That we escaped such a danger
is due to neither the moderation of the majority or
minority of that State. But compromise, both before
and after the organization of the government, over-
came the dangerous hostility to it in other States, and
by reflex action the opposition in Pennsylvania was
disarmed, and she remained the keystone State of our
national arch.

* Federalist Circular, Nov., 1788, as quoted in A. Boyd Hamilton's
Harrisburg Conference.

† Writings, I, 417.